The art of
tea-leaf reading

The art of
tea-leaf reading

JANE STRUTHERS

A GODSFIELD BOOK
www.godsfieldpress.com

For Beth, with much love

First published in Great Britain in 2006
by Godsfield Press, a division of
Octopus Publishing Group Ltd
2–4 Heron Quays
Docklands
London E14 4JP

ISBN-13: 978-1-84181-323-3
ISBN-10: 1-84181-323-0

A CIP catalogue record for this book is
available from the British Library

Printed and bound in China

10 9 8 7 6 5 4 3 2 1

Contents

Introduction

'Tea is the drink that cheers but never inebriates', claims a popular saying and tea has certainly cheered people for hundreds of years. Electricity companies brace themselves for the end of popular television programmes when demand soars because everyone has switched on the kettle for a nice cup of tea.

THE SIX TYPES OF TEA

The world of tea is much more complex than one imagines. There are over 3,000 varieties of tea, which are divided into six different types. These are black, green, oolong, white, compressed and flavoured. Compressed and flavoured teas are made from the other four types of tea, but neither is suitable for tea-leaf readings because of the way they are produced. Compressed tea is sold in blocks, with lumps broken off when you want to make tea, and flavoured tea contains tea-leaves mixed with other ingredients such as flower petals. Nevertheless, there is plenty of choice from the many black, green, oolong and white teas on the market. With so many varieties, you are sure to find something to suit your taste.

These four types of tea are picked from the tea tree *Camellia sinensis*. Incidentally, it has no connection with the medicinal tea tree plant *Melaleuca alternifolia* which produces the strong-smelling tea tree essential oil. *C. sinensis* can grow up to 18 metres (60 ft) high in the wild but when cultivated grows only to about 1 metre (3 ft) tall because it is always being picked. Herbal teas, such as raspberry leaf or camomile, do not come from this shrub and are not suitable for tea-leaf readings.

TEA-LEAF READING

Although tea is a delicious and refreshing drink, it has another dimension –
you can read the leaves after drinking your tea. You have to use leaf tea
rather than teabags, but tea made with loose leaves has a far better flavour
than that made from teabags. Tea-leaves move freely around the pot,
thereby releasing more flavour and aromatic oils into the water. And of
course loose tea provides the leaves in the bottom of your cup!

The art of reading tea-leaves, or tasseomancy, goes back thousands of
years to ancient China, when tea was first drunk. The practice developed as

a consequence of tea-drinkers interpreting the shapes of the tea-leaves that were left in the bottom of their cups and divining the future from them. When tea was first introduced to Europe during the seventeenth century it became a fashionable drink and was so popular that the meal we know as afternoon tea was introduced. This delightful interlude, involving refreshing cups of tea and dainty cakes, was a welcome innovation that broke up the day for well-to-do ladies and gentlemen who did not need to work, and they soon began to entertain themselves by reading their tea-leaves after they had drained their tea cups.

Tea-leaf reading has been popular in Europe and America ever since and is one of the easiest forms of divination to practise. All you need is a teapot, a cup and saucer, and some leaf tea, so there is no need to buy any special equipment at vast expense. You probably already have everything you need for successful tea-leaf reading in your kitchen. Reading the leaves is easy, too, because all you have to do is interpret the shapes created by the leaves when you have finished the tea.

USING THIS BOOK

This book will guide you through every stage of the tea-leaf reading process so you will feel confident about reading the leaves for yourself, for others and even for your pets. You will learn about the fascinating history of tea, as well as how to choose the most suitable teapot, cup and saucer for your tea-leaf readings. You will also discover which leaf teas are most suitable for readings, and how to divide the inside of the cup into three different time frames so that you know when the predicted event will take place. Step-by-step guides tell you everything you need to know about reading the tea-leaves, including how to read the leaves as part of a daily ritual and how to interpret them for an instant answer to a question. As well as useful guidelines on how to give successful readings for many different occasions, there is a comprehensive directory of the symbols you are most likely to find in your tea cup, divided into six categories that range from romance to careers. You will discover that tea-leaf reading is a highly enjoyable form of divination which can be a valuable guide to the future.

A short history of tea and tea-leaf reading

Life in the 21st century has become so busy that we
may not even have the time to enjoy a freshly brewed
pot of tea. If we do make a pot of tea, it is usually with
teabags because they save us having to empty out the
tea-leaves afterwards. Yet there are times when nothing
beats making tea in a more leisurely way, using the best
china, a reliable teapot and some fragrant loose tea. If
you combine this civilized ritual with reading the tea-
leaves left in your cup, you will have created a relaxing
interval in your day into which you can retreat and
enjoy some quiet reflection.

Eastern origins

People have been searching for omens and signs from time immemorial. We have studied the stars and gazed into water, as well as examining everyday objects for information about the future. The Romans used to tell their fortunes from the lees or dregs left at the bottom of their wine goblets. In a similar vein, the arrival of tea-drinking for the Chinese and Japanese was swiftly followed by the practice of reading the leaves left at the bottom of their drinking bowls.

TEA-LEAF READING

One theory states that tea-leaf reading, or tasseomancy, developed from the Chinese tradition of looking inside bells for omens. The bells were chosen because their shape was reminiscent of the dome of the heavens, and therefore drinking bowls with their rounded shapes were considered suitable for fortune-telling as well. It was certainly easier to look at a small china bowl containing a few tea-leaves than to gaze into a large bell, and the fact that the patterns in the bowl changed each time it was replenished with tea would have added to the excitement and interest.

Through the centuries, as tea-drinking became more widespread, increasing numbers of people found it enjoyable and productive to drink their tea and then examine their bowls and cups for patterns left by the tea-leaves. In an uncertain world where whole families could be wiped out by illness or famine, and where many people were at the mercy of their feudal lords, reading tea-leaves was one way of gaining some insight into what to expect from life.

THE FIRST CUP OF TEA

Many wonderful myths are associated with tea-drinking, giving it an intriguing aura of mystery. According to legend, tea as a drink was discovered in 2737 BC when the Chinese emperor Shên Nung sat beneath a wild tea tree (*Camellia sinensis*). His servant was boiling some water for his master to drink when the wind blew some of the leaves from the tea tree into the pan. Rather than remove the leaves, the emperor chose to drink the liquid. Tea drinking began. However, tea was not mentioned in Chinese literature until AD 350, when it appeared in a Chinese dictionary.

ALL THE TEA IN CHINA

Tea became the national drink of China during the T'ang dynasty of AD 618–906, and the Chinese author Lu Yu wrote the world's first book on tea in around 780. By some curious coincidence, this was also the year in which the Chinese imposed a tax on tea.

At this point, tea-leaves were steamed, crushed and formed into small cakes or bricks, which were then toasted and shredded before being steeped in salted boiling water. The Chinese word for tea was *t'e*, an Amoy dialect word pronounced 'tay'. The Cantonese referred to it as *ch'a*, pronounced 'chah'. When the tea was exported to Japan, Iran (or Persia, as it was then known), Russia and India, it was known as *chah*, while the tea exported by the Dutch to Europe was first referred to as *tay* and later as *tee*. Throughout the world, each country's name for tea originates from one of these ancient Chinese dialect words.

Buddhism was the national religion of China for centuries, and it was Buddhist priests who helped to spread tea's popularity because its moderate levels of caffeine helped them to keep alert during their meditation sessions. Tea became such a valuable adjunct to Buddhist practice that it is part of a celebrated Buddhist myth. The story goes that Bodhidharma, the founder of Zen Buddhism, was in the middle of a seven-year sleepless retreat when he began to feel drowsy. In order to stop himself going to sleep he cut off his eyelids and threw them on the ground, where they sprouted into a tea tree.

THE JAPANESE TEA CEREMONY

It is believed that tea travelled from China to Japan in the form of tea seeds carried by Yeisei, another Buddhist priest. Tea immediately became very popular in Japan, having received the seal of approval from the emperor. Its use spread to Buddhist monasteries and eventually to the general public. Drinking tea became an important Japanese ceremony known as *Cha-no-yu*, which means 'hot water tea'. It was such an elaborate ceremony that it took years of training to get it right, even though it involved nothing more than making and serving a cup of tea. Special tea-houses called *Chaseki* were built, in which the complicated tea ceremonies were performed.

At this point, the Japanese tea ceremony still had strong connections with Buddhism, but these links were gradually eroded as people began to vie with each other to create increasingly elaborate and showy tea ceremonies. This one-upmanship eventually ran its course and the tea ceremony once again became a serious and important part of Japanese culture.

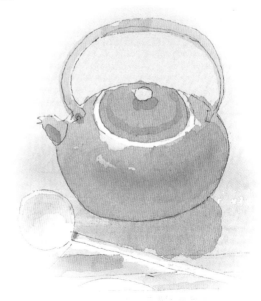

Tea comes to Europe and America

Tea was unknown in Europe until the sixteenth century when word of this curious drink spread from the Far East. The Venetians first heard about it in 1559 and the British learned of it in 1598 although they had not yet drunk it. Neither the Italians nor the British had to wait long, as the Portuguese soon began to ship tea from China to Lisbon, where it was shipped to France, Holland and the Baltic.

The popularity of tea in Europe really began in Holland, where it swiftly became a highly fashionable drink, particularly in the Hague. There was a certain amount of snob value attached to tea because it was expensive, so only the wealthiest could afford to drink it. At first tea was sold by Dutch apothecaries who also sold the expensive spices that were imported from the Orient. However, as the Dutch trade routes opened up and merchants began to import more tea, the price slowly began to drop. France also became a nation obsessed with tea, although this craze did not last there and tea was soon superseded by coffee and chocolate.

Britain is now one of the biggest tea-drinking countries in the world, and as a nation it has long believed that 'a nice cup of tea' can cure almost any ill. Yet tea did not arrive in Britain until 1657, when it first went on sale at Garway's Coffee House in London. This delay was partly caused by the disruption of the English Civil War, which lasted from 1642–49, and the subsequent national unrest and lack of money. However, in 1660 Charles II returned from his long, enforced exile, bringing with him his Portuguese wife, Catherine of Braganza, and their shared love of tea. Catherine's dowry included the ports of Tangier and Bombay, thereby increasing Britain's trade links with Africa and India. At this point, only China tea was drunk in Britain but Indian tea would gradually become equally popular.

TEA AS A LUXURY

The price of tea went up and down in the seventeenth century. In Holland, tea was on sale in ordinary shops by 1675 and no longer had the exclusive cachet it had enjoyed sixty years earlier. In Britain, tea consumption rose steadily over the years as the price dropped. However this happy state of

affairs, during which Britain developed its national love of tea, ended when the government began to impose heavy taxes on tea. Once again, tea-drinking became the preserve of the rich; by the middle of the eighteenth century the tax on tea had reached 119 per cent. Everyone wanted to drink tea although not everyone could afford to do so.

The rise of tea-drinking inspired manufacturers of porcelain and silver to produce teapots, tea cups and saucers, as well as other necessary items such as milk jugs and tea caddies. The tea caddies were often designed to hold two types of tea, and most were fitted with locks to stop servants helping themselves to the expensive contents. Many of these tea accessories spawned by the rapidly expanding tea trade have now become valuable collectors' items.

The British, ever resourceful, soon found a way round this punitive tax on their new favourite drink: smuggling. Virtually everyone, from the lord of the manor to the most lowly farm labourer, was involved in smuggling, and churches were often considered safe hiding places for the contraband. Yet, even with smuggling, tea was still an expensive pleasure, so the British began to adulterate the precious leaves with those from less valuable plants. Naturally, Parliament tried to put a stop to this and in 1725 passed a law prohibiting the adulteration of tea, with little success. Black China tea was often mixed with willow, elder or sloe leaves, and even, if times were very hard, with sheep dung and wood ash. The trade in tea-smuggling ended in Britain in 1784 when the tax on tea was reduced from 119 to 12.5 per cent. The adulteration of tea continued to be an offence, although adding sheep dung was undoubtedly still a last resort.

THE BOSTON TEA PARTY

Taxation on tea caused enough problems in Britain but no one could have foreseen the dramatic impact it would have on Britain's American colony. In the late 1640s, Peter Stuyvesant had brought tea to the settlers in New Amsterdam (later renamed New York), where it instantly became popular. Tea was first introduced to Boston in 1650 although it did not go on general sale for another 20 years.

Britain had just finished fighting the expensive French and Indian War (1754–60) to protect its new colony and needed to replenish the treasury. As a result, Britain under George III imposed a series of taxes on the colonials, including a tax on tea, much to the colonials' disgust. In December 1773 the situation had reached such an impasse that men in Boston threw all the consignments of British-imported tea into the harbour. This became known as the Boston Tea Party, and was one of the events that led to the American War of Independence in 1775. Tea is not only a pleasant drink but also an agent for revolution in the right circumstances.

Tea-leaf reading today

Just as the ancient Chinese had enjoyed reading their fortunes from the patterns of the leaves left at the bottom of their bowls, so too did the Europeans of the seventeenth century. Tea became very popular among fashionable ladies and gave rise to the new pastime of tea parties at which tea, offered with milk and sugar, was served in small, wide, handleless cups. It is easy to imagine these aristocratic ladies telling each other's fortunes by reading the leaves in their delicate china tea cups.

Over the centuries, after the end of punitive taxation, the relative price of tea fell as it became increasingly available. Tea-leaf reading continued to be popular and was especially so in times of trouble, such as the First and Second World Wars. In the meantime, tea itself had undergone a minor revolution of its own.

THE ARRIVAL OF THE TEABAG

Until the early twentieth century, the only tea available was loose leaf tea bought by weight, which could be a time-consuming business for both shopkeeper and customer. However, in 1908 a New York tea merchant called Thomas Sullivan hit on the idea of sending out samples of his tea in small silk bags. This saved having to weigh the tea out in the shop and the bag acted as a temporary tea caddy. Sullivan sent the 'bagged tea', as it was called, to local restaurants and returned a few days later to ask what they thought of it. To his astonishment, the restaurants were steeping the entire bag in boiling water to make tea for their customers rather than cutting it open before use. They told Sullivan that they liked the bagged tea because the bag allowed the tea to infuse in the pot and they saved time by not having to swill the used tea-leaves down the sink. The restaurants wanted more bagged tea. It was the birth of the teabag.

Teabags have been part of our lives ever since, and must surely rate as one of the great labour-saving inventions of the twentieth century. However, there was a stigma attached to their use because the leaves they contained were very small and graded as 'fannings' or 'dust'. What is more, customers were told not to squeeze the bags because that would release too much tannin into the cup, therefore giving a bitter-tasting drink. Tea connoisseurs frowned upon teabags because they contained unspecified blends of tea rather than tea from a specific region such as Assam or Ceylon. This situation has changed in recent years and you can now buy good-quality teabags, from reputable manufacturers, containing many popular varieties of tea.

Nevertheless, no matter how convenient teabags may be, they do not have the allure of loose leaf tea. It is a sensual experience to open a tea caddy and inhale the pungent aroma of the leaves; it is simply not the same if you peer into a caddy full of teabags. There can also be concern about whether the paper used for the teabags has been heavily bleached and whether you can taste this in the tea.

When it comes to making tea for a tasseomancy ritual, teabags are completely useless. Even if you cut them open and use the loose tea they contain, you will not get a satisfactory reading because the leaves are too small and uniform in shape. Some teabags may contain tea-leaves that are so small they float to the surface and form an unattractive brown fuzz on the top of your tea.

NEW TYPES OF TEA

The tea industry has undergone a renaissance in the past few years, with many more teas now on sale. Green tea, which was once only available from specialist tea importers, is now widely available and celebrated for its health-giving properties. You can buy many different varieties of green tea, and it has become so popular that it is used as an ingredient in some cosmetics and bath preparations.

White tea is also becoming increasingly popular. It is the rarest of the four types of tea suitable for tea-leaf reading (black, oolong and green are the other three), and therefore the most expensive. White tea is also considered to be good for one's health.

Another recent development is the manufacture of single-estate teas, which are grown and picked from a single tea-growing estate. These work on the same principle as olive oils that come from a single olive grove rather than those that come from several different suppliers and are blended at the importer's.

TEA VARIETIES AND WHERE THEY COME FROM

See the chart below for some of the most popular varieties of tea, where they come from and the type to which they belong. They are all named after the district where they are grown. Many popular teas, such as English Breakfast and Earl Grey, are blends of two or more varieties, sometimes from different countries, and are therefore not included in this list.

VARIETY	TYPE	COUNTRY OF ORIGIN
Assam	Black	India
Darjeeling	Black	India
Ceylon	Black	Sri Lanka
Kenya	Black	Kenya
Keemun	Black	China
Lapsang Souchong	Black	China
Yunnan	Black	China
Sencha	Green	Japan
Gyokuro	Green	Japan
Bancha	Green	Japan

The right tea things

Although you can read tea-leaves in the oldest and most chipped cup you own, it will add greatly to your pleasure in the entire ritual if you use a beautiful cup and saucer. You might wish to buy a special tea set purely for the purpose of tea-leaf reading, either brand-new or antique.

If you decide to buy a special tea cup and saucer for readings, you will probably want a special teapot as well. Teapots come in a wide range of shapes, sizes and colours, from reproductions of the earliest European styles to contemporary designs. If your local department store does not stock anything that appeals to you, try a specialist china shop.

The right teapot

Teapots are beautiful objects in their own right and many people enjoy collecting them. They are available in all shapes and sizes, from novelty pottery items in the shape of country cottages or animals to delicate bone china antique teapots that are worth a small fortune. Yet to most collectors it is the beauty of the teapot itself or its unusual history that is more important than its value.

As you become more adept at tea-leaf reading, you may grow to love all the objects involved, from the cups and saucers to the teapots, and wish to start your own collection. You can find many interesting examples in second-hand or thrift shops, as well as in more expensive antique shops. Another option is to attend viewings for items that are to be sold at auction, in case you spot the very thing you have been looking for.

If you are buying an everyday teapot, you will want one that pours easily and whose spout does not drip. If you always use loose tea-leaves, you might have already chosen a teapot with an internal strainer that keeps the leaves in the body of the pot and stops them escaping into your cup. You might even have bought a teapot with a special container for the tea-leaves which you can lift out after the tea has brewed to stop it becoming stewed.

Although such special teapots can be very useful in everyday life, their leaf-catching design makes them unsuitable for reading tea-leaves. Rather than use a teapot that retains the tea-leaves, you must choose one that allows the leaves to flow freely into the cup. You should also leave the tea-strainer in your kitchen drawer, even if you normally use it when pouring tea, as it has no place in the art of tea-leaf reading.

Look inside the teapot to see whether there is a metal or china strainer between the body of the pot and the spout. If there is no strainer at all, you can be confident that the teapot is suitable for tea-leaf reading. However, if there is a strainer and it is fixed in position, you must experiment to discover whether its holes are big enough to allow plenty of tea-leaves to flow down the spout. Very tiny holes will block all but the smallest tea-leaves, and will therefore restrict the scope of your readings. Ideally, the holes should be large enough to hold back some of the largest leaves but allow the others to flow through the spout into the cup.

The right cup

You might think that one tea cup is much like another and that any tea cup can be used when reading tea-leaves, but this is not true. As you become more proficient in the ritual and art of tea-leaf reading, you will develop a good eye for which cups are suitable and which are not. There are several rules to remember, especially if you want to buy yourself a special cup from which to read your own tea-leaves.

One of the most important factors is the shape of the cup. The bowl of the cup should be nicely rounded, so the tea and the leaves can move freely within it. This means that straight-sided cups (or 'coffee cans', as the small ones are called by makers of tea- and coffee-sets) are not suitable, no matter how decorative you might find them. Mugs and beakers are not suitable either. When you have found a cup with a rounded bowl, check that its interior is not fluted in any way because these undulations will interfere with the movement of the tea-leaves when you prepare the cup for a reading.

How big is the ideal cup? If it is too large, it will be unwieldy when you want to invert it over the saucer, and you may spill some tea or even drop the cup. Equally, if it is too small it may not hold enough tea, with its accompanying tea-leaves, to give you a satisfactory reading. An average-sized tea cup is your best choice, although you will also get good results with the larger size of cup known as a 'breakfast cup'.

The outside of the cup can be as highly decorated or plain as you wish, but the interior of the cup must be completely plain. Any pattern will confuse your eye and interfere with the shapes made by the tea-leaves.

These shapes should be immediately apparent and they will not be if you are unsure where the leaves stop and the pattern of the cup starts.

Look for a cup with a handle, as this is very significant in tea-leaf reading. Check that it is firmly attached to the bowl of the cup, as anything too flimsy or delicate could soon break. Finally, make sure that the cup has a matching saucer, as you will need this to catch the drips when you turn the cup upside down.

The right tea

Y ou might imagine that one type of tea is much like another, but you would be wrong. A complete world of tea is waiting to be explored and one of the most enjoyable ways to do it is through tasseomancy. You can combine the pleasure of tasting different types of tea with the insight that comes from reading the leaves remaining at the bottom of your cup. However, choose the tea-leaves carefully because some are more suitable for tasseomancy than others.

WHY SOME TEAS ARE BETTER THAN OTHERS

When choosing a leaf tea for tasseomancy, two considerations outweigh all others. The first is taste, because you will not continue with your tea-leaf readings for long if you cannot bear the flavour of the tea you are using. It might be too weak, too strong or too scented for you, in which case you will not enjoy it. So find a leaf tea that you enjoy drinking and which is suitable for tasseomancy. You may already have a favourite loose tea that works well, in which case you can continue to use it. Alternatively, you might have some enjoyable experiments ahead of you.

The second consideration is the size of the tea-leaves. They must not be too small, as in the case of some inexpensive blends of tea, otherwise they will clump together and you will find yourself trying to interpret amorphous blobs rather than defined shapes. Equally, the leaves must not be too big, as in the case of gunpowder green tea, as these will almost completely cover the inside of the cup and prevent you being able to interpret them. Ideally, the leaves should not be of a uniform shape or size, because subtle differences between them will lead to more interesting symbols being formed in the cup. Keemun tea is a good example of this as the leaves vary in size – you get small chunks as well as longer strips of leaf – and therefore produce good patterns.

Choose a tea that does not contain added ingredients, such as the tiny strips of orange peel or dried rose petals that are found in flavoured teas. This means that such delicious teas as jasmine, which contains dried jasmine petals, are unsuitable for tasseomancy.

MAKING YOUR OWN BLEND

Once you find several teas whose flavour you like and which work well for tea-leaf reading, you might enjoy combining them to create your own unique blend. Finding a good combination is largely a matter of taste, but a mixture of China and Indian black teas usually works well.

STORING TEA

Tea-leaves are delicate and need to be stored carefully, well away from any strong-smelling items that might taint them. After you open the packet of tea, store the tea-leaves in a closed container, such as a metal tea caddy or an old coffee tin (but wash it well first to remove all traces of the coffee). Do not worry if you can only find a jam jar, although you must keep it in a cool, dark place such as a kitchen cupboard.

MILK OR LEMON?

How do you like your tea? Do you always take it with milk or do you prefer to add a slice of lemon? The presence of milk in your tea will not affect the reading as most of the liquid will have drained out of your cup by then. It is entirely up to you whether you add milk to your tea, although some teas definitely taste better without it. You should never add cream to any cup of tea, purely because this will make the tea taste sickly and give it an unpleasantly thick texture. The molecules of fat in the cream may also cling to the tea-leaves, making them clump together in the cup and impair the reading.

VARIETIES OF TEA SUITABLE FOR READINGS

Listed in the chart below are some of the varieties of tea suitable for reading tea-leaves, as well as a description of their flavour. They include Earl Grey and English Breakfast, which are both well-known blends.

VARIETY	TYPE	SIZE OF LEAF	FLAVOUR
Keemun	Black	Medium	Toasted
Assam	Black	Small	Malty
Darjeeling	Black	Large	Fragrant
Earl Grey	Black	Large	Delicately scented
English Breakfast	Black	Medium	Stimulating
Ceylon	Black	Small	Full
Kenya	Black	Small	Strong
Oolong	Black	Medium	Fruity

Making the perfect cup of tea for a reading

1 Fill the kettle with fresh cold water. Just before the water boils, pour some of the hot water into the bottom of the teapot. Swirl it around to warm the pot then tip out the water.

2 Spoon the loose tea into the pot, allowing one teaspoonful for each person unless you like your tea much weaker than this. Allow the water in the kettle to come to the boil.

3 As soon as the water has boiled, pour it on to the tea-leaves in the teapot and replace the lid of the pot. Leave to stand for 3–4 minutes, stirring the tea once if you wish. The tea is now ready to be poured.

The tasseomancy ritual

When you first start to read tea-leaves you will probably feel unsure of what you are doing. However, you will find it much easier to settle into teaching yourself how to read tea-leaves if you turn the entire experience into a ritual.

When you prepare for a ritual, such as setting out a special teapot, cup and saucer for your daily tea-leaf reading, you are automatically putting yourself into a suitable frame of mind to carry out that ritual. The actions you take, such as setting a tray with the tea things and reaching for the special notebook in which you record your readings, will help to prepare your unconscious mind for what is to follow.

Preparing for the reading

Take your time when preparing for the reading. You may prefer to do this in silence, to give your mind time to settle and to put you into a suitably meditative mood.

THE RIGHT TIME AND PLACE

Ideally, you should carry out your reading when you are not distracted by anything else. Preparing for the reading will soon become almost as important as the reading itself, and it will be much easier to do this when you are not interrupted by the demands of everyday life. You might even wish to switch on your answer-phone to avoid disruption.

You may prefer to carry out your daily reading first thing in the morning so you can check the tea-leaves for information about what the day will bring. However, this will not suit you if each morning is a hectic scramble to get out of the house on time. In this case, it might be preferable to perform your daily tasseomancy ritual later in the day or when you get home from work. There are no set rules about when you should perform the ritual, so do not worry if you can only do it at lunchtime or teatime.

When choosing the right place to carry out the tasseomancy ritual, find somewhere private to avoid being interrupted by people who might ask you what you are doing, make comments about the shapes of the leaves in your cup or do anything else that will distract you or make you feel self-conscious. After you have been reading the tea-leaves for a while, you may not be so worried about what others think, and you might even welcome an audience so you can read the leaves for other people as well. You may also feel quite happy about reading the leaves in a public place, such as a tea-room or café, provided that you are served with leaf tea and not a tea-bag.

TIPS FOR CENTRING

You will not give very satisfactory readings if your thoughts are flying in several different directions at once, so it is important to centre yourself before beginning the reading. This means being able to distance yourself from your immediate concerns so you can fully concentrate on the reading. You do not want to find that part of your mind is analyzing the shapes in your tea cup while another part is wondering what to have for supper. You may find that it helps to play some soothing instrumental music in the background, such as a favourite piece of classical music (music with lyrics is not suitable because your mind will be following the words). Or you may prefer to sit in silence.

Take several slow, deep breaths, with your eyes shut. This is especially important if you are flustered or anxious before you start the reading. Picture your cares and worries disappearing with each out-breath, and

imagine a sense of peace and relaxation entering you with each in-breath. If you are unused to taking measured deep breaths, you will find it easiest if you concentrate on expelling all the air in your lungs on each out-breath because your in-breath will then automatically be deep enough to refill your lungs completely.

Keep your feet placed firmly on the floor to help ground you (see step 2 of the centring meditation below). This will help to keep you centred during the reading and enable your subconscious to work better. Repeating this grounding exercise at the end of the reading will prevent you feeling dizzy or slightly disorientated if you have been concentrating very hard.

A centring meditation

1 Choose a time and place where you can be alone. Make the tea and set the tray in front of you with your tea-reading notebook close by. Check that you have anything else you may need for the reading. If you wish, you can light a candle or nightlight, or play some soothing instrumental music. Now close your eyes and sit comfortably.

2 Place both feet firmly on the floor and imagine thick roots growing out of the soles of your feet deep into the centre of the Earth. Feel yourself being firmly anchored to the Earth and feel the energy of the Earth flowing into your body through the roots.

3 Take a couple of deep breaths, each time expelling all the air in your lungs to ensure a deep in-breath. Each time you breathe out, picture all your worries being expelled with your breath. Each time you breathe in, picture yourself being filled with bright, white light.

4 Silently ask for guidance and protection during your tea-leaf reading. Ask that all the insights that come to you will be for the greatest benefit of everyone concerned.

5 You are now ready to begin your tea-leaf reading. Open your eyes and pour out the tea.

Pouring the first cup

I f you love drinking tea, pouring out the first cup from a freshly brewed pot is always an enjoyable experience. When you are entertaining guests or making tea for friends or family, you will think nothing of pouring out several cups from a pot of tea. However, the rules are slightly different when reading tea-leaves.

WHY THE FIRST CUP IS IMPORTANT

Tradition states that you should only read the leaves from the first cup of tea that is poured out, which means that only one person can have their leaves read from each pot. Why is this? The main reason is that tea-leaves usually flow out of the pot more easily when pouring out the first cup of tea. After that, there are fewer leaves in the pot and they may stay in the pot rather than flow into the cup. Of course this depends to some extent on how strong you like your tea, because you will use fewer leaves if you prefer your tea weak.

Only reading the leaves from the first cup of tea does not matter if you live alone or are performing your tea-leaf reading ritual when no one else is around, but it can be awkward if you have invited a friend over for a mutual tea-leaf reading session. You may wish to follow tradition, in which case you should take it in turns to have a tea-leaf reading, and make a fresh pot of tea for each reading. Alternatively, if you have two teapots you could fill them both with tea to avoid having a gap between readings. On the other hand, you may like your tea strong, in which case you will be confident that there are many more tea-leaves in the pot and you can happily read the leaves

from each cup you pour. The choice is yours and you will settle on the best solution through trial and error.

Nevertheless, there is another reason why tradition insists that you should only read the leaves from the first cup. If you do not like the reading you get from your first cup of tea, you may be tempted to pour out another and try again, but this is not a good idea. It means that you are choosing to pay attention to the reading you like best and ignoring the others, which are equally valid even if they are not as propitious. If the first cup of tea produces an unsatisfactory reading, such as an undefined mishmash of shapes that have no meaning for you, or all the leaves are washed out of the cup when you invert it, it means that it is not the right time for a reading. You should try again later or the following day when the tea-leaves will probably be more forthcoming.

DRINKING THE TEA

As you drink your tea, you should try to relax. Think about the question you are going to ask the tea-leaves, if you have one, or simply concentrate on the week ahead or your life in general. Do not let your mind be distracted by current worries or mundane trains of thought. If this happens you must gently bring your focus back to what you are doing.

Drink the tea until only a small amount is left in the bottom of the cup. You are now ready to begin your reading. It is important to leave a little tea in the cup because this helps to move the tea-leaves around when you reach the next stage, which is to perform the ritual.

Performing the ritual

1 Make sure that you have drunk virtually all the tea so only a teaspoonful remains in the bottom of the cup.

2 Take the cup in your left hand if you are right-handed or your right hand if you are left-handed. Close your eyes and breathe deeply, then silently ask your question or ask for guidance about your future.

3 When you are ready, turn the cup three times in an anticlockwise direction, then turn it upside down on its saucer and leave it to drain for about 30 seconds.

4 When you are certain that all the tea has drained into the saucer, carefully turn the cup up the right way. You are now ready to interpret the shapes of the tea-leaves in the cup.

Reading the leaves

Before reading the leaves, spend a few moments quietly looking at them and tuning in to them. This will enable your subconscious to get to work, picking up on the atmosphere around you and also on the energies being produced by the tea-leaves. Practice makes perfect, so do not expect instant success. It may take time to get used to reading the leaves, especially if you find it hard to identify the shapes they make. If they do not seem to make any sense, turn the cup round in case they have a more recognizable shape from another angle. It will also help to squint when looking at the leaves, as this will increase the contrast between the dark shapes of the leaves and the paler colour of the cup.

First impressions

Your initial impressions of the arrangement of the tea-leaves in the cup are important because they may give you essential information that you might otherwise overlook. When you first begin to read tea-leaves, you may long to rush straight into an in-depth reading rather than taking time to assess the shape and distribution of the leaves first. Your readings will be more successful if you can be patient enough to see what impressions come to you before you even look at the cup.

CENTRING YOURSELF

When you are ready to give the reading, take several deep, regular breaths in order to achieve a state of calm balance. If you are agitated or nervous, you will not be able to tune in to any sensations that are conjured up by the shapes of the leaves. It will help to follow the centring meditation (see page 39) before you begin the reading. Clear your mind of any preconceived ideas about the reading or the questions that have been asked, especially if the reading is being given in a time of crisis, and do not try to guess what the tea-leaves will tell you. Aim to feel centred within yourself, in an alert yet relaxed state, so you will notice any change in your emotions when you look into the cup.

Now take the cup in your hands, but you should not look into it at this stage. Are you registering any emotions that do not belong to you, such as panic, elation or trepidation? Take note of any feelings that come to you because they may be a useful indicator of the state of mind of the person for whom you are giving the reading.

LOOKING INTO THE CUP

You are now ready to look inside the cup. Resist the temptation to immediately begin analyzing the shapes of the leaves, but simply gaze at them instead. If there are several groups of leaves within the bowl of the cup, which ones catch your attention first? Does one group seem more important than the others, even if it is smaller or less distinct than everything else? For instance, a small question mark that is formed by the leaves may seem more important to you than the bigger shapes.

Are you experiencing a particular sensation that does not seem to belong to you now that you are looking at the leaves? Take note of all these feelings and impressions but do not to jump to any conclusions at this stage. Your intuition may also tell you whether any of the shapes should be read literally, or symbolically or whether they may form some sort of visual pun. For instance, a fan shape might suggest an encounter with an admirer.

Dividing the cup into sections

Mentally divide the bowl of the cup into three sections in order to read the leaves more efficiently and determine the time frame to which they belong. Also take note of any patterns of tea-leaves that appear near the handle, as this is a very significant area of the cup.

THE HANDLE

This part of the cup represents you or whoever is receiving the tea-leaf reading. Traditionally, you always read the tea-leaves in a clockwise direction, starting to the left of the handle. Patterns of tea-leaves that appear close to the handle describe events or emotions that have a direct effect on the person who is having the reading. For instance, the pattern might describe an aspect of this person's character or something that is on his or her mind at the time of the reading. However, you must determine whether the pattern falls to the right or left of the handle, because its position indicates the time frame in which it occurs. The area immediately to the left of the handle represents the past and the influences disappearing from the person's life, while the area immediately to the right represents the present and the future.

THE THREE AREAS OF THE BOWL

The bowl of the cup is divided into three sections, each representing a particular time scale. The rim and upper third of the cup refer to the immediate present and the next couple of days. The middle section of the cup represents the relatively near future, usually up to two weeks away. The

lower third of the cup and the base of the bowl represent between two and four weeks away.

This means, for instance, that if the tea-leaves form the shape of a cat near the base of the cup, the person having the reading will enjoy a stroke of good luck (the meaning of the cat symbol) within the next two to four weeks. A heart shape near the rim means the person will have an emotional encounter within the next two days. As you become more practised at reading the tea-leaves you will find it easy to gauge the time frame.

Basic steps in reading the leaves

Reading the leaves is not nearly as daunting as you might think if you have never tried it. You simply need to trust your intuition and examine the symbols you see in the cup, combining their meaning with the position they occupy in the cup and the nature of the question. You will become much more proficient as you continue to practise tea-leaf reading, so do not let yourself become despondent if the first few sessions do not yield much information. Everyone has to start somewhere. Nevertheless, you can take various measures to ensure that your readings are as good as possible.

ASK THE RIGHT QUESTIONS

To ensure success at reading tea-leaves, make sure you ask the right questions. Try to keep your questions as simple as possible to make it easier to find the answers within your tea cup. You will only confuse yourself if you ask a multiple-choice question, such as 'Should I go on holiday with my best friend or would it better if I stayed at home and saved the money?' When answering a question like this, you might find tea-leaf shapes that refer to whether or not you will go on holiday, your best friend, your home and your finances, and it will not always be clear what each shape refers to. It is better therefore to either ask one question per reading (such as 'Should I go on holiday?') or to ask for guidance about your current circumstances and see which areas of your life are described by the tea-leaves.

If you ask a specific question, such as the one about whether you should go on holiday, look at the area nearest the handle first because this section refers directly to you. If you cannot find anything here, look in the rest of the cup for the answer.

If you ask for general guidance look at the area around the handle first, but be more open-minded when interpreting the shapes you find here. There could be a few surprises about what they refer to, so you should not try to limit their relevance to things you already know about or for which you need guidance. Make a note of what you see here, even if it makes no sense at the time, because it may become obvious later on.

LOOKING AT SHAPES IN THE RIGHT ORDER

Sometimes you will only have one shape to interpret in the tea cup, but at other times you will be presented with many different shapes. When this happens, which ones should you interpret first?

A simple rule of thumb is to start with the largest shapes and then to work systematically down to the smallest. You should also take a few moments to look at the cup without interpreting the shapes, so you can get a feel for it and the messages it contains (see page 47). When a cup is full of shapes, it means that the questioner is experiencing an important phase in his or her life.

MOISTURE IN THE CUP

Before starting a reading you always invert the cup over its saucer and leave the remaining tea to drain out before turning the cup up the right way again to begin the reading. Normally, this allows all the tea to drain into the saucer, but sometimes it gets trapped between the tea-leaves and remains in the cup when you come to read the leaves. Tradition says that moisture in the bottom of the cup represents tears and sorrow, and that these are usually present in the questioner's life at the time of the reading. You may therefore want to examine any symbols in the upper third of the cup in great detail, to gain more insight into the cause of the sorrow. However, do not frighten the questioner into thinking something awful is going to happen.

Reading the leaves

1 After performing the ritual of preparing the cup for the reading (see page 43), you are ready to read the leaves. Pick up the cup and hold it in your hands, but do not look into it yet. Sit quietly with your eyes closed and notice any emotions or impressions that come to you.

2 Open your eyes and look into the cup. Note the general distribution of the tea-leaves within the cup. Are they evenly arranged throughout the three sections of the cup or they are mostly contained in one of the sections?

3 Now look at the shapes of the leaves, starting with the largest and begin to interpret them. Are there any other shapes near them that might give you further clues about their meaning? If so, try to combine these meanings to give them a coherent link, rather than reading each one separately.

4 Look for shapes that are linked together in some way, such as two animal shapes, because these will give further credence to your interpretation of them.

Recording readings

It is always interesting to record your tea-leaf readings because you will want to refer to them later on to check their accuracy. You will also enjoy looking back over your interpretations to see how, with practice, you have developed and become more skilled.

A SPECIAL NOTEBOOK

The best way to record your readings is to write them down in a special notebook, which can be an inexpensive exercise book or a beautifully bound journal. Do not write anything else in it, such as shopping lists or phone messages. Keep this special notebook with your tasseomancy teapot and tea cup so it is always ready when you need it. Make sure you keep a pen or pencil with it so you do not have to go searching for one when you are ready to begin your tasseomancy ritual. Such distractions can be irritating and occasionally might mean that you get caught up in some other task while searching for a pen and forget all about giving yourself the reading.

When using your notebook to record your readings, it is helpful to allow space to include your later feedback of the reading. One way to do this is to allocate a double-page spread for each reading. Write the time, date and place of the reading at the top of the left-hand page, plus any other useful information such as the variety of tea you are using. Then write down your question or request for guidance, followed by the answers and the time scale to which you think they refer. Instead of simply noting the shapes that you see, such as an umbrella, a dog and a building, you should also write down your interpretations of them. Write these as fully as possible, because once you start writing all sorts of ideas may come to you that later turn out to be much more pertinent than you imagine at the time.

Only write on the left-hand side of the double-page spread, and continue on the next left-hand page if necessary. Leave the right-hand pages blank for the moment, because you will be coming back to these later on.

Revisit your interpretation of the reading a couple of weeks later, so you can check it for accuracy. Have any of the events you predicted come true? Even if you did not interpret them as accurately as you would have liked, can you see a link between the shapes formed by the tea-leaves and the events that took place? On the right-hand side of the page, write down whether your predictions have come true and, if not, whether there are links between your predictions and what did happen.

The etiquette of giving readings to others

How do you give someone else a reading? This is very simple, although there are a few guidelines to remember. Normally, if you are giving a reading for someone in your own home, you will probably be the one who makes the tea and sets out the tea tray. If you give someone a reading in their own home, that person will probably make the tea. If you are not sure whether he or she will have a suitable variety of leaf tea, you might like to bring a little loose tea with you. You can always say that it is the special tea you use for readings if you are worried that your host might be offended in some way. You must also reassure this person that what passes between you will remain confidential, especially if you have friends in common.

GETTING COMFORTABLE

Before the reading starts, you should both be comfortable and relaxed. A reading in which you can take your time and be left alone is likely to be much more successful than one in which you are surrounded by noisy chaos. If you are in someone else's home it may be difficult to do anything about this without sounding rude. Even so, you should try to create as relaxing an atmosphere as possible so you can give a good reading and the other person is in a suitable mental state to listen to what you say.

POURING THE TEA

It does not matter who pours the tea, but your friend might like to do it if he or she is receiving the reading. Remember, the first cup is traditionally the most important, so this should be given to your friend. Encourage your friend to drink the tea while thinking about the question he or she wants to ask the tea-leaves. When your friend is ready, guide him or her through the tasseomancy ritual and then ask him or her to hand the tea cup to you, so the reading can begin.

SOME GUIDELINES

When giving someone a reading, always bear in mind that the person will be paying a great deal of attention to what you are saying even if he or she appears to treat the whole thing as a joke. Do not be unduly negative or alarmist or use the reading as an opportunity to give your friend the benefit of your advice. Simply describe what the tea-leaves are saying, and ask if this has any relevance for him or her. If it does, you can develop your theme. If it does not, do not panic, because the significance of what you are saying may become apparent later on. Sometimes, the reading acts as a chance for your friend to talk about whatever is troubling him or her, so do not be surprised if what you thought would be a short reading turns into a longer and more complex conversation. Try to allow enough time for this eventuality so you do not have to watch the clock obsessively.

Readings for every purpose

Try to get into the habit of recording your readings by writing them down in your special notebook and sketching the images formed by the tea-leaves. After you have become a proficient tea-leaf reader, you can confidently start to read the leaves for other people, as well as give yourself special readings to answer specific questions. Be receptive to the messages that the tea-leaves have for you, and use them as an opportunity to examine your life whenever this is appropriate. If you take them seriously you will find that they respond by giving you serious answers to the questions you ask.

Tea-leaf reading as a daily meditation

O ne of the most rewarding ways to read tea-leaves is to incorporate the process into your daily routine. You can check the leaves in private or when you drink your first cup of the day. If you wish, increase the sense of private ritual by using a special teapot, cup and saucer. Do not allow anyone else to use these tea things and put them away after use.

PREPARING FOR THE DAY AHEAD

A morning reading can provide information about what the day ahead will bring or give you specific help with the events of the day. If you have an important meeting or social engagement, ask for the reading to concentrate on that event. Alternatively, if you are worried about something that will happen that day, such as a doctor's appointment or a job interview, ask about the outcome or for guidance on how to deal with whatever happens.

It may take some practice to tune into the subtle message of the leaves. Doing a reading each day, whether or not something important is happening, will develop your intuition and give you insight into yourself. Make sure you read the leaves objectively rather than try to fit the reading to the outcome you want.

To help you refine your analytical skills, record your daily reading in a journal or notebook and follow up your morning notes each evening with comments about what happened and the accuracy of the reading. Sketch what you see in the cup to create your own directory of personal symbols and their meanings.

A morning reading

1 Prepare the cup in the usual way (see page 43). Try to create a sense of calm even if you are worried about the day's events. If you wish, use the meditation on page 39 to relax and centre yourself. Focus your mind on the question you want to ask.

2 If you have asked for guidance about a specific issue, examine the cup for the answer. If you have asked for general guidance about the day ahead, be receptive to the shapes formed by the leaves.

3 Consult the directory of tea-leaf symbols (see pages 72–123) for the meanings of the shapes.

Tea-leaf reading to answer a question

There will be times when you want the tea-leaves to answer a particular question, perhaps concerning your family or your love-life. This is different from simply asking the leaves for guidance about the day ahead or a specific problem; in this case you want them to answer your question and you must interpret the leaves accordingly.

PHRASING THE QUESTION

It is important to keep your question as simple as possible. If you make the question too complicated, you will be expecting too much from the leaves and the messages you get may be confusing. You may also wonder which tea-leaf shapes refer to which part of your question if it is too complex.

LOOKING FOR AN INSTANT ANSWER

Sometimes, you will want to ask the tea-leaves a simple question that requires a 'yes' or 'no' answer. However, the leaves are unable to spell out such words so you must devise another way for them to give you an instant reply. One method is to perform the tasseomancy ritual in the usual way (see page 43) and then to look inside your cup for symbols that have an obvious 'yes' or 'no' meaning. For instance, symbols such as a smiling mouth, a star or a heart give a 'yes' answer, and symbols such as a down-turned mouth, a cross or a cloud give a 'no' answer. You may find that the cup contains a symbol that describes the subject matter of your question. For instance, if you ask whether you will have a child and the tea-leaves form the shape of a baby, this will be a 'yes' answer.

An instant answer reading

1 Make the tea and drink it, keeping your question in mind. When you are ready to begin the reading, ask the question either aloud or silently then prepare the cup in the usual way (see page 43). Take some deep breaths so you feel relaxed and at ease.

2 Look inside the cup for answers to your question. Can you see any shapes that have a positive meaning and which could give you a 'yes' answer, or any shapes that have a more negative connotation and could therefore be a 'no'? Or are there any shapes that relate to the question itself? Look up the meanings of the shapes in the tea-leaf directory (see pages 72–123).

3 Record the answers, whether easily understood or uncertain, in your special tea-leaf-reading journal. If you did not get a clear-cut answer, try again another day.

Categories of readings

You can ask the tea-leaves questions about any topic, from everyday matters to once-in-a-lifetime events. The directory of tea-leaf shapes in this book (see pages 72–123) will give you an excellent starting point for interpreting many of the images you will find when reading tea-leaves.

The directory of tea-leaf shapes is divided into six categories: career; romance; family and friends; money and values; health; and travel. These categories have been chosen because they feature heavily in most people's lives. What follows are some useful tips when interpreting the symbols for each of the categories. Some apply specifically to one category and other tips may apply equally well to the other categories or to other areas of life not covered here that you will wish to explore during your own readings.

YOUR CAREER

When giving yourself a reading about your career, or doing one for someone else, always keep in mind the sort of situations that might arise. These involve dealing with colleagues, bosses, employees, being self-employed, wanting promotion, wanting to switch jobs to something more fulfilling or better-paid, being very ambitious or coping with unemployment. If you bear such considerations in mind when reading the leaves, you will always be able to find some connection between the symbol in the cup and the career-focused question. Alternatively, the symbol may be a pun. For example, finding a bow in the cup may mystify you at first. Does it mean a bow-tie or a ribbon tied in a bow? If neither of these interpretations means anything to you, think of other meanings of the word. Perhaps it means taking a bow, as

in receiving the plaudits due to you after a successful piece of work.

If you are still uncertain about what the symbol might mean, look through the other categories in the directory in case they contain something very similar or they trigger your intuition and give you an answer.

Finally, if giving the reading to someone else and you do not understand some of the symbols in the cup, do not be afraid to ask the person concerned if these symbols make sense to them. He or she might tell you that the puzzling symbol is part of their company's logo or that it sounds like a boss's name.

ROMANCE

If giving yourself a reading about a romantic question, one of the most important points to remember is not to be so focused on getting the 'right' answer that you ignore what the symbols are telling you. For instance, if you want to know whether you will marry the person you are currently in love with, you may be tempted to ignore the three disappointing symbols in your cup and persuade yourself that the amoeba-like blob is actually a bell, and therefore that wedding bells will ring out for you. Comforting though this might be at the time, you will be fooling yourself in the long run and events will prove that the disappointing symbols were correct and the vague bell shape was misleading.

Sometimes you need additional information when interpreting some symbols that appear in your cup, especially if you are not sure to whom they refer. If you can clearly see a pair of lips in your cup, symbolizing a kiss, but you are currently single, you may wonder who will be giving you the kiss. Examine the shapes near the pair of lips in case they give you more information. For instance, you might find an initial letter, which will hint at the name of the person concerned, or a symbol that acts like a visual pun. To give an example of how this could work, you might see a key near the lips, and remember that you recently met an attractive man or woman whose surname is Key. Could this be your mystery kisser?

FAMILY AND FRIENDS

When interpreting the tea-leaves for family and friends, think about how they may react to what you tell them. You may have to touch on subjects such as family gatherings (which may be fraught or happy), parental

expectations, anxieties about children, news of babies, meeting new friends, falling out with friends and many more. These situations can be very emotionally charged and you must remember this when giving someone a reading about this area of his or her life. Choose your  words carefully when describing what the tea-leaves say about a family situation or a particular friend in order to avoid giving offence or sounding as though you are taking sides.

Bear in mind when giving a reading about someone's family and friends that the person's situation may mirror your own experiences but you should not let this fact colour your reading. In other words, do not project your own emotions or opinions on to that person because he or she may have an entirely different attitude towards the situation.

Look for initials, which will help you to identify people referred to in the reading. You may also see astrological symbols, which tell you the person's Sun sign. For instance, a lion may represent a Leo or a ram might refer to an Aries.

MONEY AND FINANCE

Money can be a source of great anxiety, so bear this in mind when asking questions about your finances. You may be so worried about getting a favourable reading that you ignore any warnings given by the leaves and concentrate on the more encouraging symbols instead. If you are giving a reading for someone else about monetary worries, try to keep your own financial situation separate and not allow it to colour the reading. For instance, if you are going through a very lean phase financially and the tea-leaves indicate that your friend will soon be receiving a windfall, you must keep any pangs of envy to yourself.

When asking questions about money you can expect to see money-related symbols in the cup. These will include the symbols for different forms of currency, such as British sterling and the American or Australian dollar. You can also expect to see numbers, as these can give information about the amount of money involved or the amount of time that will elapse before the money arrives.

HEALTH

Be very careful when giving readings connected with health, whether for yourself or someone else. This is especially true if you have no medical expertise, so do not be tempted to give dire prognostications or to talk about things of which you have no experience.

If you do see a warning sign in someone's cup, you must pass on the warning without scaring this person out of their wits. You might ask the person how he or she is feeling or suggest that a trip to the doctor for a check-up might be a good idea, but that is all. If you see a symbol that really worries you about your own health or that of the person for whom you are giving the reading, it will always be supported by other negative symbols. It may also appear in several readings. If you are worried about your health you should always seek medical advice. Tasseomancy readings should never be used in place of a medical consultation.

TRAVEL

As always, when interpreting readings that concern
travel bear in mind the sort of situations you are likely
to encounter. These can include such pleasant
experiences as excitement about the journey, happiness
at reaching the destination and the thrill of going on the
holiday of a lifetime, as well as more difficult ones such as coping with travel
delays, mix-ups over tickets, worries about air travel, finding lost luggage and
trying to make yourself understood in a foreign language.

The shapes you see in the cup may represent forms of travel, such as a
train or car, but sometimes they will have a symbolic meaning. For instance,
a bicycle may represent a journey that you take alone and a train may signify
a journey in the company of others, with someone else in charge.

Special readings

As you become more accustomed to reading the tea-leaves you will realize how versatile this form of divination can be. Not only can you read the leaves to discover the major concerns of your day ahead or to ask a particular question, you can also consult the leaves about special occasions. Here are some suggestions for expanding your tea-leaf reading skills.

READINGS FOR PETS

If you have a pet, there will inevitably be occasions when you would like some insight into her emotional or physical welfare. Sit in the same room as the animal (or outdoors if that is more appropriate) while you drink the tea and think of your question, so you begin to tune in to your pet's energy. After turning the cup three times anticlockwise and inverting it over the saucer, you can gently place it next to your pet so it connects with its energy. Most cats and dogs will sniff the cup or nudge it with their noses, which is their way of participating in the reading.

You can now read the leaves in the usual way. Examine the cup for symbols that point to whatever is troubling your pet. Although such readings can be very informative if your pet is ill or out of sorts, they should never be a substitute for getting a proper diagnosis and treatment from your vet.

READINGS FOR SPECIAL DAYS

Some days, such as birthdays, are special and therefore deserve a special reading. If it is your birthday, you could conduct your daily ritual reading in the usual way but ask for information about what the coming year will

bring. Record the symbols and your interpretations in your special notebook so you can refer to them during the months ahead. You can follow the same procedure on any other special day, such as your wedding day.

READINGS FOR MOVING HOUSE

Moving house is one of the most stressful events in most people's lives, so do not hesitate to ask the tea-leaves for guidance. If you have yet to find a new home you could ask the tea-leaves to describe the sort of place you should be looking for or the area in which you will find it. In this case, you will have to interpret some of the symbols literally. For instance, if you see a mountain in your cup it may mean that you will move to a mountainous area.

Tea-leaf directory

This section consists of a directory of the symbols you are most likely to find in your tea cup. It is divided into six sections, which cover the areas of life that usually concern people the most, ranging from personal relationships to career and health.

When you are ready to read your tea-leaves, you should identify the shapes you find in your cup and then look them up in this part of the book to discover their meaning. If the shape you find in your cup does not match any of those you find here, do not be afraid to use your intuition when deciding what its meaning might be. If your interpretation turns out to be accurate, you could jot it down for future reference.

Using the Directory

The variety of symbols you can expect to see in your cup is endless, and ranges from the simple to the complicated. This directory will help you to interpret them.

THE SIX CATEGORIES

The directory is divided into six everyday categories: career; romance; family and friends; money and values; health; and travel. These have been chosen because they are the areas of life that most of us are concerned about and which might therefore be the focus of your tasseomancy readings. Reading the interpretations in each category will give you a good grounding in what the symbols mean, so take the time to understand and absorb them.

As you read through the list of symbols you will discover that some have quite literal meanings while others have more abstract interpretations. Nevertheless, each symbol has been interpreted according to its basic meaning in the light of the category in which it is placed. If you think about the meaning you will always see some connection between the symbol and its interpretation. This will show you how to marry the nature of the question with the meaning of the symbol. It will also enable you to develop your tea-leaf reading skills still further by thinking about the meanings of any symbols that are not listed in this book but which appear in your cup. If you see a symbol with special meaning for you that is not mentioned in the directory, trust your instincts about which interpretation is correct for the reading.

SAME SYMBOLS, DIFFERENT CATEGORIES

As you read through the list of symbols in each category, you will notice that some shapes appear only once while others crop up several times. For instance, it is quite common to find a bell shape in your tea cup but it will have a different meaning according to the nature of your question.

Therefore, a bell may mean wedding bells or some other celebration if your question concerns romance, but it can signify an important message when it refers to your career. If you cannot find the symbol you want in the category that describes your question, look for it in the other categories to discover its basic meaning. You can then adapt that meaning to fit the category you are dealing with.

FINDING NEW SYMBOLS

As you become more skilled at reading the leaves and interpreting their shapes, your intuition will begin to guide you about the meanings of shapes that are not listed in this book. If you allow your intuition to flow, rather than block it through anxiety or a belief that you are not 'special enough' to receive intuitive guidance, it will become increasingly reliable. Keep practising reading the tea-leaves, whether for yourself or others, because this will improve your confidence.

Career

Here are some of the symbols you will come across during the course of a reading about your career.

Ladder

You are climbing the career ladder and doing well. Beware of being complacent or of ignoring people who have helped you on the way up.

Snake

You have hit a difficult patch in your career and there will be an unexpected change in your status. How can you learn from these disappointments and get back on track?

Star

You are about to achieve a special ambition that feels like your heart's desire. This is a very favourable sign, especially if you are currently going through a testing phase.

Moon

People and situations are not what they seem, so treat them with caution. Do not believe everything you are told or only listen to one side of an argument.

New moon

This is a time for new beginnings. It is excellent for launching a new project connected with your career or for looking for a new job. You are filled with hope and confidence.

Comet

This is a very favourable symbol because it shows that you are blazing a trail in your career. If your working situation has been difficult recently it will soon undergo a transformation.

Closed circle

You are about to reach the end of one cycle and the start of another. One area of your career is over and there is no going back. Be prepared to look ahead to the future.

Straight line

You are going through a rather tedious, predictable phase. Are there any symbols nearby to show that a change is on the way or are you stuck with the status quo for the time being?

Chair

A chair indicates the arrival of a new colleague, boss or client. Examine any nearby symbols to see if this is an enjoyable relationship or one that will bring problems.

Square

Your progress is blocked and you must find ways to overcome this frustrating experience. Look in the cup for nearby symbols that will show how to move forward. If there are none, you must be patient.

Acorn

This is a very positive sign because it shows the small beginnings of a project or opportunity that will grow and develop over the years. Nurture it well in its early stages.

Mountain

You are facing a major challenge. It may seem so daunting that you wonder how you will cope. Take it slowly. Remember the saying 'a journey of a thousand miles starts with the first step'.

Bicycle

Cultivate an independent attitude and do not rely too much on others. This is a phase in which you must go it alone. Have faith in your abilities and in your stamina.

Pen

You will soon have to write a letter or sign an important contract. Check its contents carefully for accuracy and make sure its meaning is clear and not misleading in any way.

Airplane

This symbolizes one of two things. It can either mean that you will be taking a long journey or that you will meet someone who comes from overseas.

Clock

This indicates an important meeting or appointment. Look at the symbols surrounding the clock for indications of whether this meeting will be a success.

Dots

A line of dots indicates the arrival of money. This could be in the form of a pay rise, a better-paid job or a bonus. If the dots are close to another symbol, this will give more information about where the money comes from.

Arrow

Is the arrow pointing up or down? An upward-pointing arrow is a good sign as it shows that your circumstances are improving and things are looking up. A downward-pointing arrow shows a temporary setback.

Cloud

Something connected with your career is not yet visible or has yet to be explained properly. Wait for this to be revealed and in the meantime do not make assumptions about what it might be.

Egg

This is a very fertile stage in your career because
something is hatching. Nurture this project or opportunity
carefully until it is well established.

Baby

This is a very promising symbol to appear in your cup
because it shows fresh possibilities and the start of
something new. Look for nearby symbols that will give
you more information about what this might be.

Bee

A bee foretells a very busy and productive phase,
especially if you will be working with others. This is
a good time to concentrate on establishing the basic
structure of a project.

Bell

An experience or person will act like a wake-up call.
This might alert you to possibilities you have
overlooked until now or remind you to concentrate on
the essentials. Be open to the message you receive.

Flag

Take care because this flag is giving you a warning about
something. Perhaps you should take more care when
handling a certain person or a project, or you are getting
out of your depth.

Hat

Promotion is on the way. This is a very favourable symbol
because it shows you are being taken seriously at work,
and that people appreciate all the efforts you are making.

Anchor

When it describes your career, an anchor has a mixed message. It tells you to create as much stability as possible but without starting to feel bogged down and unable to move forward.

Axe

You are facing a struggle in which you must hack your way through something. This will call for determination and resolution as well as the courage of your convictions.

Boat

Does the boat look stable or is it at an angle? A stable boat is a good sign because it shows your career is going well. A boat at an angle shows you are entering stormy waters.

Crown

A crown is a very positive and encouraging symbol because it indicates success, applause and increased self-esteem. It is especially encouraging if you are seeking promotion.

Dagger

Take care because someone cannot be trusted. They may be jealous of your success or about to betray you. Or are you the one who wants to stab someone else in the back?

Open square

This symbol describes new beginnings. You are being offered the chance to start again with a clean slate. This might mean a new job, a relocation or, if other symbols support it, an entirely new career.

Eye

You are being warned to become more aware of what is going on around you. You may be missing some good opportunities simply because you have not noticed them yet.

Gate

Is the gate open or shut? If it is open, new avenues are opening up for you. If it is shut, you will have to revise your strategy and approach your goals from a new direction.

Wheel

Congratulations, because you are making progress and things are going well. Nevertheless, there will be times when you must alter your pace in order to adapt to your circumstances.

Key

This is a very positive symbol because it shows that new doors are opening in your career. Once you start to follow the right path, many opportunities will present themselves.

Lion

You will receive help from an influential friend or associate. They may be in a position of power, so they can pull strings for you. A lion also shows that you should take pride in your work.

Scales

Are the scales in balance? If so, you have things in proportion. If not, something in your career is out of balance and must be adjusted. Perhaps you are working too hard?

Umbrella

If the umbrella is open, it shows that you will be given some form of protection. If it is closed, it indicates that something is hidden from you and has yet to be revealed.

Face

Someone is playing an important role in your career, whether they are a colleague, boss or client. Look for nearby symbols that describe how this person will affect you.

Spiral

You are going round in circles, which is a waste of your time and effort. However, it is difficult for you to know how to change the situation or get back on track.

Exclamation mark

Prepare for a surprise. Look for nearby symbols to discover what sort of surprise this will be. If there are no symbols, the surprise will have a big impact on you.

Question mark

A question mark is hanging over one aspect of your career, creating a sense of mystery or frustration. Do your best to avoid misleading others, whether intentionally or accidentally.

Shark

Take care because someone has adopted a predatory attitude towards you. They may be after your job or they may want to intimidate you, so protect yourself as best you can.

Zigzag

Someone is expecting you to do things in a predictable or obvious way, but you want to take a more individual approach. Follow your instincts but do not be deliberately controversial.

Train

You are making good progress, especially if you are working in conjunction with other people. There may be occasional setbacks but you will eventually reach your goals.

Horse

This is a very encouraging symbol because it shows that you have strength and dignity. It can sometimes indicate that you must work as part of a team.

Lighthouse

A lighthouse is a sign of guidance and advice. Whether you will be giving this guidance or receiving it, its content will help to avert danger as well as less serious problems.

Sun

When you find a sun in your cup, it is telling you to have faith and confidence in yourself. Trust in your abilities and do not be unduly modest about them. You need to shine.

Cup

Is the cup the right way up? If so, it shows that you are being offered a valuable opportunity. If the cup is upside down, what you are offered will turn out to be worthless.

Sword

A sword usually warns of clashes and arguments in which you will have to protect yourself. Sometimes, it can also describe worries that are overwhelming.

Romance

Here are some of the symbols you will come across during the course of a reading about romance.

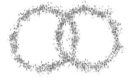

Two rings
This is a very favourable symbol because it either describes a new relationship or a union of some kind. This could be an engagement or wedding, or something else that brings joy.

Hook
Someone has got under your skin, making it difficult for you detach yourself from him or her whether you want to or not. Do not let this relationship turn into an obsession.

Heart
This is a time of complete emotional fulfilment and happiness. Your love is reciprocated and your relationship looks strong, whether it is platonic or sexual.

Damaged heart
Someone has hurt you badly. Despite this, the relationship is not over yet and can be saved if you are willing to repair the damage. Try not to harbour injured feelings.

Broken heart
A relationship is finished and there is no going back. You must accept the situation, painful as it is, because it cannot be changed. Allow yourself a period of mourning.

Triangle

You are involved in a three-way relationship. Someone or something is competing for a loved one's attention or affection.

Chain

There is a strong emotional link between you and someone you care for. Work hard at strengthening this bond because it will bring you happiness.

Wall

There is a barrier, either physical or emotional, between you and someone else. It will take a lot of effort and strength of will to overcome it.

Dog

Demonstrate your affection and devotion towards your loved ones. This is a good opportunity to show how loyal and faithful you can be, especially if someone needs your support.

Fan

You have an admirer. However, this person may have an idealistic image of you that is based more on wishful thinking than on reality.

Butterfly

Someone is flirting with you. You must decide whether the person means what he or she says or is simply playing a light-hearted game.

Exclamation mark

Someone is behaving in ways you did not expect. You may not like what the person is doing but that does not necessarily mean that you have the right to ask them to behave differently.

Question mark

You are mystified by the way a certain person is behaving. Is the person playing a game with you? Look for other symbols nearby which will explain what is going on.

Scales

Your emotions are operating like a see-saw, swinging up and down. This is exhausting for you and makes you constantly on edge. Think about what is bothering you so much.

Fireworks

A relationship is very exciting, whether it appeals to you on a mental, emotional or physical level. It is an intoxicating experience and you cannot get enough of it.

Hat

Someone wants you to play a different role in their life. You might go from being friends to lovers or vice versa. Are you ready for this change and do you have any control over it?

Cross

This is a warning symbol because it indicates conflict with someone. It is not easily solved but it will help to be adaptable and to admit to the part you have played in the situation.

Lips

A pair of lips describe a kiss, but who is doing the kissing? It might be an existing partner or lover, or it could be someone you have yet to meet. A nearby exclamation mark shows there is a surprise involved.

Sword

This is a difficult time emotionally, caused by betrayal,
mistrust and mischievous gossip. Someone may be involved in
a fight with you for another's affection.

New moon

A new moon is always a positive sign for romance. It either
indicates a new relationship or a new phase in an existing
partnership. Sometimes it shows the need for forgiveness.

Hourglass

If you have been meaning to get in touch with
someone, do not delay because time is running out.
They may not wait to hear from you for much longer.

Ribbon

When you find a ribbon in your cup it describes a gift. You
may be the lucky recipient or you might be the donor.
Sometimes the gift is connected with a celebration, such as
a birthday.

Lightning

A flash of lightning signifies a sudden realization. Perhaps you
have reached a startling conclusion about someone or they
have made an important discovery about you.

Scissors

This is an unfortunate symbol for romance
because it describes some form of division.
This could be a separation between loved
ones, temporary or permanent.

Spoon

Be on your guard because someone is doing their best to stir up trouble. They may be spreading rumours or gossip, or sowing seeds of doubt in someone's mind.

Rainbow

This is a very positive symbol because it shows that a cherished wish will come true. However, do not expect it to happen without any input from you.

Nest

A nest is a happy sign because it describes settling down with someone. In other words, you are in a nest-building mood and will enjoy a happy domestic life.

Face

This is a very encouraging symbol if you are feeling lonely because it shows that someone new is about to enter your life. There will be a strong romantic attraction between you.

Swan

Swans mate for life, so this symbol represents a long-term, happy and settled relationship. It is a good sign if you are wondering whether to make an emotional commitment to someone.

Owl

An owl carries a warning about betrayal and disappointments. You should be careful about who you trust, but equally do not become suspicious of everyone's motives.

Tree

This is always a positive symbol, and when it refers to romance it is telling you to allow a relationship to grow. You will be able to depend on the person concerned for support and love.

Mushroom

If you find the shape of a mushroom in your cup, it is telling you that a particular relationship must be allowed to develop at its own pace. Do not rush it or force it.

Full moon

When referring to romance, a full moon describes a critical time in a relationship. Problems must be sorted out and there is the need for a workable compromise.

Pansy

A pansy shows that someone is thinking of you. Are there any symbols nearby that will tell you what this person is thinking, or why they are so concerned about you?

Spade

You are in danger of digging yourself into a hole when you find a spade in your cup. Are you getting too involved with someone or have you told a white lie that is now getting out of hand?

Fence

If the fence is intact, it shows that you are separating yourself from someone special. Is this intentional or do you want to increase your contact with them? If the fence is broken, it will be much easier to re-establish your connections with this person.

Dove

If you have had a row with someone or there is some other rift between you, a dove is a very favourable sign because it describes peace after quarrels. Perhaps you should be the first person to say sorry?

Wine glass

A wine glass describes some form of celebration, and when it is linked to romance it could indicate an engagement party or wedding reception.

Whale

Watch out, because you are about to be consumed by your passion for someone. This may be exciting at the time but it could make you lose your sense of perspective.

Fish

A fish is telling you to trust your gut feelings and follow your intuition, especially if you are wondering how to behave with a certain person. Your instincts will tell you what to do.

Bell

You have something to celebrate. It could be a wedding, especially if the bell is accompanied by a wine glass or a heart. Sometimes a bell can mean you will receive an important telephone call from someone.

Envelope

An envelope traditionally indicates the arrival of a letter, such as a love letter, although it could now describe a romantic e-mail as well. Whatever it is, it will make you happy.

Sunrise

This is a very encouraging symbol, especially if you have been going through a difficult phase, because it describes a new relationship or the rebirth of an existing one.

Tank

Be careful when you find the shape of a tank in your cup because it means you are going into battle with someone. There will be arguments and conflict, but is it a cause worth fighting for?

Bridge

This symbol is encouraging you to create a rapprochement with someone. Rather than harbour grudges, do your best to forgive the other person and build bridges between you.

Key

Someone has more impact on you than you realize. Perhaps you have given them the key to your heart and they are now going to unlock some of your innermost secrets.

Arch

This symbol always describes an opening. This could be a way forward, especially if you are currently in a difficult situation. Look for a way through your current troubles.

Bee

A bee is a positive symbol and when connected with romance it describes a happy and productive time. Sometimes it can describe a special holiday, such as a honeymoon.

Crab

Someone is being clingy and needy. Is this you or a loved one? If you are behaving like this, try to find the root cause of this emotional insecurity and then do something about it.

Wavy lines

These indicate a difficult time in a relationship, with many ups and downs. Look at the neighbouring symbols to see what has caused this erratic phase and whether it is serious.

Family and friends

Here are some of the symbols you will see during the course of a reading about family and friends.

Stars
A group of stars indicates a happy home life. This is an especially favourable sign if you are setting up home with someone or buying property.

Table
This symbol indicates a family celebration or a big gathering. Enjoy the chance to be together and take pleasure in one another's company.

Nest
This is a very auspicious symbol because it describes the ability to create a happy home life, whether you live alone or with others. It can also indicate a house move.

Full moon
There will be a change in your domestic circumstances when you find this symbol in your cup. You might move house or you could finally resolve a family problem.

New moon
A new moon always represents the beginning of something. Therefore, there could soon be a new member of your family, such as a child. This is also a good time to make some improvements to your home.

Telephone

A telephone indicates an important message, either to or from a friend or relative. It might arrive by telephone but instead it could be sent by fax or e-mail.

Basket

This symbol represents a gift for your home or family. It may be a physical object, such as a moving-in present, or it could be something less tangible, such as a happy experience for everyone concerned.

House

This is telling you to concentrate on your home life, especially if it has had to take second place to other demands on your time, such as work commitments.

Cat

It is important for a loved one to express their independence, even though this may fill you with misgivings about their welfare. This person must be allowed to go his or her own way.

Clock

You need to spend time with older members of your family. Ask them about the past and enjoy listening to their reminiscences. You might hear some interesting information.

Chair

You will have a visitor. If there is an exclamation mark nearby, the visitor is unexpected or unwelcome. Sometimes a chair indicates a new member of the family.

Tree

A tree is telling you to strengthen your family roots. You might do this by spending more time with your family or by revisiting childhood haunts. Be open to the emotions that result from this.

Dragon

The dragon sends a mixed message because it describes upheavals and difficulties. However, these will eventually have a positive outcome.

Wine glass

This cheerful symbol is encouraging you to do some entertaining. You might throw a big party or may only want to hold a small gathering, but either way it will be enjoyable.

Dagger

This dagger comes as a warning because it is telling you that someone close to you cannot be trusted. Treat them with caution and do not let them get the better of you.

Ear

You will hear some interesting news about someone close to your heart. This news may come to you through a third party or the person concerned might want to confide in you, in which case you should listen carefully to them.

Fox

Someone is wily and crafty. At best, they are unreliable. At worst, they are untrustworthy. Be careful, especially if the fox is accompanied by other difficult symbols.

Mouse

This represents an intrusive or uninvited visitor. Alternatively, it can describe someone who is inquisitive, timid and nervy, and who needs to be handled gently.

Fish

If you only find one fish in your tea cup, it hints at a house move. If you find two fish, it can describe someone who was born under the sign of Pisces. Look for a nearby initial to see who this might be.

Flag

Flags are often flown as a warning, and this flag is telling you that someone cannot be trusted. Take care that they do not lead you into trouble, whether by accident or design.

Clouds

You are beset by temporary problems about loved ones when you find clouds in your tea cup. The good news is that these problems will eventually disappear.

Hand

Someone is offering you the hand of friendship, but do you want to take it? A nearby initial or other symbol will offer clues about this person's identity and intentions.

Bowl

This is a marvellous symbol because it shows that you are being offered something of great emotional value. Treasure it and be thankful to receive such a gift.

Anchor

When it appears in a reading concerned with friends and family, an anchor denotes stability and security. However, take care that this comfortable situation does not lead to complacency.

Gate

Is the gate closed or open? If it is closed, there are obstacles in your relationship with a certain person. If the gate is open, you will soon follow a new path with them.

Ant

Ants are very industrious creatures that spend a lot of time making their nests, so this ant is telling you to make changes and improvements to your home or domestic arrangements.

Bee

This symbol is encouraging you to spend time with your family and friends. This might involve arranging a special get-together for people you do not see very often.

Clown

Someone dear to your heart is putting a brave face on their problems. They may be laughing them off in public but feeling scared in private. Try to encourage them to talk to you.

Ivy leaf

An ivy leaf is telling you that old friends are very important. Make an effort to get in touch with some of them, particularly if you live far away from each other.

Kettle

This is a positive symbol because it represents a happy home life. This is very encouraging if you are thinking of starting a family or moving house.

Mermaid

In myths, mermaids lure sailors into the deep, and therefore tea-leaves in the shape of a mermaid describe someone with a negative influence or mischievous intentions.

Boat

When you find a boat in your tea cup it means that your dreams will give you guidance. Perhaps you should write them down when you wake each morning so you can remember them.

Key

When it relates to your family and friends, a key is a classic indication of a change of address. Are you the one who is moving house or is it a loved one?

Lamppost

If you can see a lamppost in your cup, it shows that someone needs your guidance. Literally, they would like you to shed light on something that is bothering them.

Rose

Here is a very positive symbol because a rose signifies great happiness. It is the sort of happiness that comes from being with the people you love and which is very precious.

Pig

This is a happy symbol because it is telling you that someone is trustworthy and faithful. You can depend on them to help you through difficult times.

Apple

This symbol is telling you not to give in to temptation. What sort of temptation is it? It could be the temptation to be unkind to someone or to overlook their needs, particularly if helping them seems too difficult a prospect.

Eye

This is a very encouraging and sustaining image because an eye is a sign of protection. Someone is watching over you, whether you are aware of their concern or not.

Tea pot

This symbolizes an important meeting with some of the people you care about. It might be an occasion on which you really do use a tea pot or an event in which you share other things besides food and drink.

Cherry

A cherry represents a productive, fruitful and happy phase, so it is always a welcome symbol. It is especially favourable if you are thinking of moving house or beginning a family.

Wings

A set of wings tells you that an important message will arrive from a far-off place. It may come in an airmail letter or a long-distance telephone call. Sometimes it arrives in an otherworldly dream.

Baby

Babies represent birth, whether literal or metaphorical. So a baby in your cup means the birth of a child, the start of a new domestic project or the blossoming of a productive relationship.

Cow

This is a particularly reassuring symbol if you are thinking of moving house or making other changes to your home life because the cow represents peaceful contentment. All will be well.

Four-leafed clover

A four-leafed clover is valuable because it is so rare. The presence of one of these rarities in your cup brings the promise of a special kind of happiness that not everyone can experience.

Exclamation mark

When you see an exclamation mark describing your family and friends, it is telling you to expect the unexpected. There are surprises in store from loved ones.

Crab

This symbol has two meanings. It can either describe someone who is born under the sign of Cancer, in which case a nearby initial may help to identify them, or it shows that a loved one is being defensive and difficult.

Bell

If you find a bell in your cup it means you will have a visitor. Is this someone you are expecting or will the arrival take you by surprise? Look for nearby symbols that can give you more information.

Spiral

When the tea-leaves are arranged in a spiral they are telling you that history is repeating itself. Is this something to rejoice over or is it a cause for concern?

Comb

Be on your guard because someone will turn out to be a false friend. They might deceive you in some way or they may let you down when you need them the most.

Diamond

A diamond foretells news of an engagement. This is usually a cause for celebration, especially if you can see a wine glass nearby. However, you may not be so happy about the engagement if the diamond is accompanied by a less positive symbol.

Money and values

Here are some of the symbols you will see during the course of a reading about money and values.

Currency symbol
A symbol of currency, such as the US dollar or British sterling, is an encouraging sign because it shows that money is on its way. It may not be a fortune, but at least it is something.

Balloon
This shows that you will be going up in the world, probably through an increase in your prosperity or status. Do not let this go to your head – make sure you stay grounded.

Four-leafed clover
This is always a very positive symbol and when it appears in a reading connected with money it describes happiness and prosperity. It can also mean the ownership of something rare and valuable.

Anchor
An anchor is telling you to make financial decisions that are solid and grounded in reality. This is especially important if you are involved in a property deal.

Spider
Traditionally, a spider promises that money will soon be arriving. Very often, it comes through a stroke of luck, such as a winning lottery ticket or a prize in a competition.

Magnifying glass

This has a cautionary message because it is telling you to read the small print of a contract or agreement very carefully to ensure it does not contain mistakes or clauses that will work against you.

Vase

This symbol advises you to search for the value in something. This may mean finding more meaning in your daily life if you have become disenchanted with it recently.

Hourglass

This is a warning sign because it is telling you that financial delays will be costly. For instance, you should make sure your mortgage or credit card payments are up to date.

Clouds

Clouds always carry a cautionary message, and when connected with finance they are telling you that there is some sort of problem looming. Sort it out as quickly as possible.

Telephone

Do your best to avoid confusion and misunderstandings by being as clear and straightforward as possible. Do not evade problems by sitting on the fence or telling fibs.

Lamp

It is time to shed new light on an old worry connected with your priorities in life or your finances. Look at the problem from a different angle and without letting panic cloud your judgement.

Sheep

Sheep are renowned for their herd-like instincts, and this symbol is telling you not to follow other people's advice blindly because it may not be right for you. Think for yourself!

Bee

The bee is often a benign symbol but when connected with finances it is telling you not to let someone sting you. You should also take care not to trick others in any way.

Ant

The more industrious you are, the better your finances will be. This is no time to be lazy or to expect good fortune to land in your lap. You will reap what you sow.

Butterfly

Keep track of your financial position and do not fritter your money away on trivial purchases and impulsive whims, especially if you are feeling bored or restless.

Kite

This symbol shows that you have big financial goals, but will you attain them? If you can see a tail on the kite it shows that you stand a good chance of being successful.

Fountain

This is a very encouraging symbol because a fountain promises happiness and contentment. You will have everything you need for a fulfilling life.

Jug

Share and share alike. Do not keep your money or possessions to yourself because it is far better to share them with the people who need them.

Fork

You are being presented with more than one choice, but which should you take? Look for adjacent symbols that will give you more information about which option to choose.

Hammer

When you find the symbol of a hammer in your cup it is telling you to persevere at something. You must be determined and persistent.

Nest

A nest means you must be prudent, farsighted and save some money for the future. Perhaps you should save up for something really enjoyable?

Dog

Dogs are renowned for their loyalty and this symbol is encouraging you to be faithful to your plans of improving your finances. Do not give up.

Egg

This is the start of a new phase in your finances or values. Maybe it is time to concentrate more on your priorities in life?

Loaf of bread

This symbol describes a phase when money is thin on the ground. Although times are hard you will survive if you are prudent.

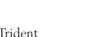

Trident

Do not confuse reality with wishful thinking, especially if there is a vast gulf between the two. Face the financial facts, no matter how painful they might be.

Hook

Keep your wits about you and do not let someone fool you or trick you out of your money, regardless of how plausible their story sounds.

Car

Watch out, because you are being taken for a ride. Someone is doing their best to part you from your money or possessions, and you must be on your guard.

Foot

Keep your feet firmly on the ground when handling your finances. Be sensible and careful, and then all will be well. This is not a time to take risks.

Parachute

Is the parachute intact? If so, it is telling you that a financial risk will pay off. However, you should not pursue this risk if the parachute is damaged.

Scales

These always show a need for balance and here they are describing your financial position. If the scales are level, your finances are good. If they are uneven, your money will fluctuate.

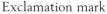

Pen

This describes an important letter or document connected with something of value. Have you written it or will you receive it? Either way, it will have a greater significance than you imagine.

Exclamation mark

This symbol is urging caution by telling you not to make impulsive decisions about your possessions or finances. It is far better to play safe to avoid nasty surprises.

Throne

A throne is a very encouraging symbol because it indicates promotion and success. Such benefits may bring you a monetary bonus or they may represent emotional satisfaction instead.

Basket

You will be taking several shopping trips when a basket appears in your cup. You will enjoy spending money but make sure you know when to stop.

Umbrella

Give yourself financial protection by putting aside some money for a rainy day. Try to get into the habit of being a regular saver.

Acorn

Mighty oaks grow from little acorns and this fortunate symbol is advising you not to be afraid to start small. This may involve a modest investment that will grow in value.

Musical note

You will receive some money when you find a musical note in your cup. Look for a nearby number to give you clues about how much money this will be.

Hand

Is the hand pointing towards another symbol or a different part of the cup? If so, the hand is drawing your attention to this area. If the hand is not pointing anywhere, it shows that fate is taking a hand in your life.

Mushroom

This is a very encouraging symbol, especially if you are going through a lean time, because it describes increased prosperity and good fortune.

Grapes

A bunch of grapes represents abundance, whether this is emotional fulfilment or financial gain. Grapes can also indicate monetary reward after some hard work.

Arrow

This is a very good symbol if you are going through an indecisive or uncertain phase because it is saying that you will soon be shown which direction to take in life.

Ear

Listen out for some interesting and informative news connected with your finances. You might receive some good advice about what to do with your money.

Cage

Be careful because a proposal or offer that seems good will turn out to be a very different proposition. It may trap you in some way or dramatically reduce your options.

Feather

This age-old symbol is saying that you will be judged by your actions so you should be very careful about what you are doing. Try to be honest and above reproach.

Scissors

You must trim your expenses and outgoings to fit your income. This is not a good time to live on credit or beyond your means.

Ship

This is a very positive symbol because it shows that you will soon be better off, whether financially, emotionally or spiritually.

Watch

Timing is everything when the symbol of a watch appears in your cup. Is this a good time for making financial moves or should you wait for a more favourable phase?

Barrel

This positive symbol indicates a period of abundance and plenty. Enjoy it and try to make sure others share in your good fortune.

Window

This shows that you need to cultivate vision and foresight when dealing with your finances. Look beyond the immediate future and short-term gains to the bigger picture.

House

This is an encouraging symbol to find if you are thinking of investing your money in property because you will do well, provided that you make sensible decisions and do not take foolish risks.

Health

Here are some of the symbols you will come across during a reading on the subject of health.

Saucepan
This symbol is telling you to pay attention to your diet and general nutrition, especially if you have been skipping proper meals recently.

Elephant
An elephant is a positive symbol because it denotes good health and general wellbeing. It is also telling you to take life at a leisurely, relaxed pace.

Bed
The symbol of a bed means you should get plenty of rest. Perhaps you have been burning the candle at both ends and now you need to recuperate?

Pillow
Dreams are a vital way of receiving messages from our subconscious, and a pillow is telling you to pay more attention to your dreams. Maybe you should start recording them in a special notebook?

Pipe
You have been rushing around and it is now time to relax and take life easy for a while. Retreat from life's hurly-burly and enjoy some quiet meditation by yourself.

Ship

Listen to your unconscious because it is speaking to you through your dreams and your instincts. To deny it is to deny part of your self.

Airplane

When describing your health, an airplane tells you that you need a holiday. You might literally want to fly off into the wide blue yonder, or you may only have time for a weekend away. But you do need a change of scene.

Hairbrush

The symbol of a hairbrush means that a change of image will boost your energy and sense of self-worth. This is especially important if you have been feeling fed up or tired.

Spring

This suggests that you are lacking in energy and need to increase your vitality. Seek medical help if the situation does not improve.

Feather

This feather is telling you to check that you are the right weight. It can also indicate a phase in which you lack direction and purpose.

Apple

An apple a day keeps the doctor away, according to an old saying, and this apple is suggesting that you should consult a doctor over any health worries you may have, no matter how minor they seem to you.

Ear

This ear is telling you to listen. Perhaps you will be given some excellent advice about your health or maybe someone needs to confide in you about something that is troubling him or her.

Spoon

When it is describing your health, a spoon suggests that you may need to change your diet. Are you eating any foods that you know do not agree with you?

Wavy lines

These lines indicate fluctuating levels of energy, making you feel up one moment and down the next. How can you improve the situation?

Star

This is always an encouraging symbol and when connected to your health it says that things will get better. It can also indicate a period of convalescence after an illness.

Wine bottle

This wine bottle has a simple meaning because it describes the need for temperance, not only over alcohol but also where your general diet is concerned.

Cup

For true health, you must do something that refreshes your spirit. This could be anything from taking regular walks in the countryside to starting a daily meditation practice.

Dog

This symbol is encouraging you to take more physical exercise. Build up your stamina gradually and avoid going to extremes.

Horse

You are stronger than you think, both mentally and physically. Nevertheless, you should not push yourself further than the limits of endurance.

Bee

You are living on too much nervous energy and you need to relax more. Try to slow not only your body but also your mind, otherwise you will exhaust yourself.

Bird

How much interest do you take in your immediate surroundings? Make an effort to appreciate the little things in life as well as the bigger events.

Scales

You need to find a better balance between work and play because your personal scales are weighted too far in one direction at the moment.

Question mark

Something is worrying you and you are expending a lot of energy on it. You will not feel better until you have solved the problem.

Leg

Do you lead a sedentary life? This symbol is telling you to be more active and to incorporate more exercise into your daily routine, even if it is only a walk round the block.

Smiling face

You need to be more positive. You are taking life too seriously and this sombre attitude is eroding your energy levels. Do something that will help you to lighten up.

Sun

This is a very positive symbol because it represents resurgence and revival. It is especially encouraging if you are recovering from a bout of ill health because it promises that you will soon feel better.

Cloud

Do not let worries affect your health. Confide in someone you trust if you need to discuss your problems, or do something constructive to help solve them. But brooding on problems does not help.

New moon

This is a sign of fresh starts, and it is telling you to take a new approach to your health and diet. Get professional help if you cannot do this on your own.

Tree

A tree sends its roots deep into the soil for nourishment, and this symbol says that you need to become more in tune with nature in order to nourish your soul. Spend time out of doors.

Four-leafed clover

This very happy symbol tells you that a wish will come true. Perhaps a health worry will disappear or you will discover a way of life that gives you more energy and improves your wellbeing.

Broom

New brooms sweep clean, and this broom is encouraging you to make a fresh start in connection with your health. Bring an end to a bad habit, such as smoking, and notice the positive impact this has on the rest of your life.

Knife

This brings news of an operation, injection or surgical procedure. You may be the one who will undergo it or it could be someone close to you.

Daisy

This is a symbol of hope, health and vitality. It is especially welcome after a period of illness or exhaustion, particularly if accompanied by a sun or a star.

Anchor

This anchor is saying that you need more stability in your life. Perhaps you need to establish a more settled routine or some facet of your life has got to change for the better.

Candle

You need more rest because you have been burning the candle at both ends. Try to take life at a less hectic pace, especially if you crave having some time to yourself.

Snail

You need to become more like a snail and slow down. At the moment you are trying to cram too many activities into too small a time frame, and it is wearing you out.

Butterfly

They say that variety is the spice of life, but do you have enough variety in your own life? Try to become more flexible, adaptable and open to doing things on the spur of the moment.

Hand

You need a helping hand. This could come from someone who will give you support or guidance, or it may arrive in the form of a massage or some other bodywork.

Cross

This symbol always carries a warning, and here it is telling you to take care of yourself and seek help about anything that is worrying you.

Key

This is an encouraging symbol because it says that a health problem will be solved. This is especially good news if a mystery of some kind has surrounded your ailment.

Plus sign

This shows that you need to add something to your life. What could this be? Is it more exercise, more fresh air, better food or more rest? A nearby symbol in the cup may give you more clues.

Lines of dashes

These lines denote a very busy time in which you are dashing from one activity to the next, with barely a chance to pause for breath. Try to slow down whenever you get the chance.

Sheep

Be patient and do not get anxious about things over which you have no control. Do your best to adopt a more contemplative and placid approach to life.

Ladder

This is a positive symbol because it says that your health and general vitality will improve. However, they will not do this on their own so you must give them a hand by taking better care of yourself.

Barrel

Keep a close eye on your weight and try to reduce the intake of foods that are not good for you. Be particularly careful not to rush to the fridge when you are bored or in need of comfort.

Scissors

Scissors cut things, so what do you need to cut out of your life in order to improve your health? Seek medical advice if you intend to make some dramatic changes.

Fan

Do not get in a flap about the things that do not really matter and which distract you from more important issues. Learn to reduce the level of anxiety in your life.

Heart

Spend time with people you care about because you will benefit emotionally and physically from their company. Be prepared to give love as well as to receive it.

Broken heart

Someone has hurt you badly. Your heartache is depleting your energy and making you feel listless. Look for adjacent positive symbols to remind you that you will gradually start to feel better.

Bowl

This is a very positive symbol because it shows that you will be offered an opportunity that will benefit your health in some way.

Travel

Here are some of the symbols you will come across during the course of a reading about travel.

Horse

This symbolizes a journey that you will take by yourself and at your own pace. The trip will benefit you in some way, whether professionally, emotionally or physically.

Coach or bus

This represents an organized journey with other people, in which someone else is in charge. It will be enjoyable but it may be a struggle to get on well with all your fellow passengers.

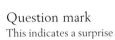

Kite

A kite describes an unexpected journey, often taken at the last minute or on a sudden whim. Look for a nearby initial or other clue to tell you more about your destination.

Question mark

This indicates a surprise connected with travel. Nearby symbols will reveal more about what the surprise entails, but will not tell you the whole story.

Suitcase

Spend time planning a journey or holiday because all the preparation will pay off. Try to be as organized as possible, and check that you have everything you need for the journey.

Palm tree

This symbol describes travel to another country, especially if it has a hot climate. This is more likely to be a journey taken for pleasure than one for business purposes, unless adjacent symbols tell a different story.

Straight lines

Rows of lines are a classic sign of journeys and a busy time generally. You might take several long-distance journeys or many short trips, but either way they will involve a lot of time.

Cloud

Clouds often have negative meanings but when they appear in a reading about travel they signify a journey by air. Adjacent symbols will tell you more about this journey.

Diamond

This is a very encouraging symbol to find in your cup because it means that a journey or trip will bring big rewards. These may be emotional, spiritual or financial.

Anchor

There will be delays to a journey when an anchor appears in your cup, so be patient. Sometimes the anchor describes a journey taken by sea, especially if you can see a boat symbol nearby.

Mountain

This shows that you will take a spiritual journey. It may involve physical travel or it may be purely emotional or mental, but it will be of great benefit to you.

Cat

A cat shows that you will be going on a short journey. Good fortune may be involved in some way in this.

Shell

Are you thinking of taking a trip to the seaside? It will be enjoyable and restful. Alternatively, a shell may mean that you will be travelling over water.

Fan

You will be involved in a flirtation while you are taking a journey. This may be nothing more than fleeting fun or it could be much more serious. Look for nearby symbols that give more information.

Bicycle

A bicycle means that you will be taking a short journey by yourself. However, if it is a tandem it means that someone will accompany you on this journey.

Clock

Allow plenty of time when travelling by public transport or in your car in case you encounter irritating delays or setbacks that make you late.

Zigzag

Be prepared for last-minute changes of plan to a travel itinerary. You must do your best to go with the flow and adapt to changing circumstances.

Face

You will meet someone important on your travels. He or she could be a complete stranger or you may already know them, but they will certainly make a big impact on you.

Musical note

A journey or holiday will be harmonious and enjoyable. If you travel alone, you will meet some convivial companions en route.

Bird

You will be taking a short journey by yourself. This will be valuable because it will give you a fresh perspective on your life.

Flock of birds

This shows that you may be thinking about emigrating to another country. Alternatively, you will enjoy going on holiday with friends.

Cup

You will be taking a trip that involves a celebration. Perhaps this is a journey to a wedding or a special family occasion, or maybe the celebration will come as a complete surprise.

Zebra

This symbol describes adventure in a foreign country. It may also be encouraging you to take a holiday in an exotic location.

Star

A star is always a positive symbol and when it refers to travel it describes a trip that will turn out much better than you had hoped.

Hourglass

Before you travel, check the day and time on your tickets to ensure that they are correct. You should also avoid leaving any travel arrangements to the last minute.

Trident

This trident is telling you to soak up the atmosphere of a place you will be visiting, especially if you will be going there for the first time. Tune into it as much as possible.

Bee

You will have a full itinerary during a journey that you take. Try to find the time to relax in between all your other activities.

Ant

Make the most of the opportunity to take a journey involving your work or a favourite pastime. The length of the journey is less important than what you get out of it.

Angel

The symbol of an angel brings you good news about someone who lives a long way away. You may be seeing them sooner than you think.

Chair

You will be taking an unexpected journey. You may also have a surprise travelling companion. Look for adjacent symbols that give you more information about this.

Square

You are facing some awkward obstacles in a travel plan. These difficulties must be overcome before you can take things any further.

Parallel lines

Parallel lines symbolize a journey that you will take either by rail or by road. Are there any symbols nearby that will tell you more about this trip?

Chain

When you find a chain in your cup, it is telling you that a journey will lead to unexpected developments and new connections, whether on a personal or professional level.

Comet

This is a very auspicious symbol because it indicates that you will be taking an exciting, successful and momentous trip. It may lead to increased prestige for you.

Lighthouse

This describes travel to a destination that you have never visited before but which will be very significant for you. It will be a memorable trip.

Candle

A mystery surrounds a journey, whether it is taken by you or a loved one. This journey may have a mystical or spiritual significance.

Human figure

You will have an important encounter with a stranger during a trip or holiday. Look for nearby clues, such as an initial, for more information about this person.

Elephant

It is said that elephants never forget and this symbol shows that you will have a memorable experience while travelling. Look for nearby symbols that will give you clues about what this might be.

Triangle

This shows that you will meet three special people or have three important experiences while on a journey or holiday. Be open to whatever happens to you.

Key

A house move will involve a journey for someone. Perhaps they are relocating to another part of their country or they are emigrating.

Wheel

You are going through a time of immense change, and one element of this will concern a journey of some kind. This might be a physical journey but it could involve travel of the mind instead.

Baby

A trip will lead to the birth of something new. This could be a relationship, a job or an opportunity that would otherwise have passed you by.

Car

This is a classic indication of a journey, although not necessarily by car. If you can see parallel lines nearby, these show that it will be a long journey.

Telephone

In a reading about travel, a telephone signifies an urgent summons from afar. You may be asked to take a trip at short notice, so be prepared.

Ski

This indicates an enjoyable holiday, which may or may not involve winter sports. Nevertheless, it will probably be an active holiday in which you are kept fully occupied.

Star

This has two meanings. It shows either that you will go on a quest for something deeply significant to you, or that you will travel to a place you have always wanted to visit.

Rocks

You will have to deal with small problems and minor hitches while travelling. This will be a nuisance but they are nothing to worry about.

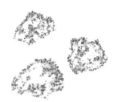

Dice

Do not take chances or trust to luck because the odds are not in your favour and things will not work out in the way you want. Play by the rules and avoid foolish risks.

Full moon

This describes a nostalgic journey, perhaps to a destination that has a lot of emotional significance. Enjoy the memories but do not let yourself live in the past.

Basket

This is a very favourable symbol if you are going on your travels because it says that you will return with more than you had when you left.

Index

Acknowledgements

Writing this book has been a very enjoyable experience and I would like to thank everyone who has been involved in it. Heartfelt thanks to everyone at Godsfield who worked on it, but especially to Brenda Rosen, who is a joy to work with, my editor Charlotte Wilson and Jennifer Barr. And thanks, too, to my agent, Chelsey Fox, and to my husband, Bill Martin, for all their help, encouragement and support.

Executive Editor Brenda Rosen
Editor Charlotte Wilson
Executive Art Editor Sally Bond
Designer Janis Utton
Illustrator Nicola Gregory
Production Manager Louise Hall